Connected  Mathematics™

Clever Counting

Combinatorics

Student Edition

Glenda Lappan
James T. Fey
William M. Fitzgerald
Susan N. Friel
Elizabeth Difanis Phillips

Prentice
Hall

Glenview, Illinois
Needham, Massachusetts
Upper Saddle River, New Jersey

Connected Mathematics™ **was developed at Michigan State University with the support of National Science Foundation Grant No. MDR 9150217.**

This project was supported, in part,
by the
National Science Foundation
Opinions expressed are those of the authors
and not necessarily those of the Foundation

The Michigan State University authors and administration have agreed that all MSU royalties arising from this publication will be devoted to purposes supported by the Department of Mathematics and the MSU Mathematics Education Enrichment Fund.

Photo Acknowledgements: 12 © Michael J. Olonlewski/The Image Works; 13 © Ann and Myron Sutton/FPG International; 22 © Geoffrey Apple; 34 © Miro Vintoniv/Stock, Boston; 38 © Nick Dolding/Tony Stone Images

Many of the designations used by manufacturers to distinguish their products are claimed as trademarks. Where those designations appear in this book, and the Publisher was aware of a trademark claim, the designations have been printed in initial caps or all caps.

ISBN 0-13-053085-9
5 6 7 8 9 10   05 04 03

The Connected Mathematics Project Staff

Project Directors

James T. Fey
University of Maryland

William M. Fitzgerald
Michigan State University

Susan N. Friel
University of North Carolina at Chapel Hill

Glenda Lappan
Michigan State University

Elizabeth Difanis Phillips
Michigan State University

Project Manager

Kathy Burgis
Michigan State University

Technical Coordinator

Judith Martus Miller
Michigan State University

Curriculum Development Consultants

David Ben-Chaim
Weizmann Institute

Alex Friedlander
Weizmann Institute

Eleanor Geiger
University of Maryland

Jane Miller
University of Maryland

Jane Mitchell
University of North Carolina at Chapel Hill

Anthony D. Rickard
Alma College

Collaborating Teachers/Writers

Mary K. Bouck
Portland, Michigan

Jacqueline Stewart
Okemos, Michigan

Graduate Assistants

Scott J. Baldridge
Michigan State University

Angie S. Eshelman
Michigan State University

M. Faaiz Gierdien
Michigan State University

Jane M. Keiser
Indiana University

Angela S. Krebs
Michigan State University

James M. Larson
Michigan State University

Ronald Preston
Indiana University

Tat Ming Sze
Michigan State University

Sarah Theule-Lubienski
Michigan State University

Jeffrey J. Wanko
Michigan State University

Evaluation Team

Mark Hoover
Michigan State University

Diane V. Lambdin
Indiana University

Sandra K. Wilcox
Michigan State University

Judith S. Zawojewski
National-Louis University

Teacher/Assessment Team

Kathy Booth
Waverly, Michigan

Anita Clark
Marshall, Michigan

Julie Faulkner
Traverse City, Michigan

Theodore Gardella
Bloomfield Hills, Michigan

Yvonne Grant
Portland, Michigan

Linda R. Lobue
Vista, California

Suzanne McGrath
Chula Vista, California

Nancy McIntyre
Troy, Michigan

Mary Beth Schmitt
Traverse City, Michigan

Linda Walker
Tallahassee, Florida

Software Developer

Richard Burgis
East Lansing, Michigan

Development Center Directors

Nicholas Branca
San Diego State University

Dianne Briars
Pittsburgh Public Schools

Frances R. Curcio
New York University

Perry Lanier
Michigan State University

J. Michael Shaughnessy
Portland State University

Charles Vonder Embse
Central Michigan University

Special thanks to the students and teachers at these pilot schools!

Baker Demonstration School
Evanston, Illinois

Bertha Vos Elementary School
Traverse City, Michigan

Blair Elementary School
Traverse City, Michigan

Bloomfield Hills Middle School
Bloomfield Hills, Michigan

Brownell Elementary School
Flint, Michigan

Catlin Gabel School
Portland, Oregon

Cherry Knoll Elementary School
Traverse City, Michigan

Cobb Middle School
Tallahassee, Florida

Courtade Elementary School
Traverse City, Michigan

Duke School for Children
Durham, North Carolina

DeVeaux Junior High School
Toledo, Ohio

East Junior High School
Traverse City, Michigan

Eastern Elementary School
Traverse City, Michigan

Eastlake Elementary School
Chula Vista, California

Eastwood Elementary School
Sturgis, Michigan

Elizabeth City Middle School
Elizabeth City, North Carolina

Franklinton Elementary School
Franklinton, North Carolina

Frick International Studies Academy
Pittsburgh, Pennsylvania

Gundry Elementary School
Flint, Michigan

Hawkins Elementary School
Toledo, Ohio

Hilltop Middle School
Chula Vista, California

Holmes Middle School
Flint, Michigan

Interlochen Elementary School
Traverse City, Michigan

Los Altos Elementary School
San Diego, California

Louis Armstrong Middle School
East Elmhurst, New York

McTigue Junior High School
Toledo, Ohio

National City Middle School
National City, California

Norris Elementary School
Traverse City, Michigan

Northeast Middle School
Minneapolis, Minnesota

Oak Park Elementary School
Traverse City, Michigan

Old Mission Elementary School
Traverse City, Michigan

Old Orchard Elementary School
Toledo, Ohio

Portland Middle School
Portland, Michigan

Reizenstein Middle School
Pittsburgh, Pennsylvania

Sabin Elementary School
Traverse City, Michigan

Shepherd Middle School
Shepherd, Michigan

Sturgis Middle School
Sturgis, Michigan

Terrell Lane Middle School
Louisburg, North Carolina

Tierra del Sol Middle School
Lakeside, California

Traverse Heights Elementary School
Traverse City, Michigan

University Preparatory Academy
Seattle, Washington

Washington Middle School
Vista, California

Waverly East Intermediate School
Lansing, Michigan

Waverly Middle School
Lansing, Michigan

West Junior High School
Traverse City, Michigan

Willow Hill Elementary School
Traverse City, Michigan

Contents

Clever Counting

A locker at a storage warehouse was robbed. The police suspect that the thief tried possible lock combinations until the lock opened. A lock combination consists of three numbers from 0 to 39, with no repeated numbers. How many combinations are possible?

A witness saw a white van speed away from the scene of a crime. He said the van had in-state license plates starting with the letters MTU. License plates in the state where the robbery took place contain three letters followed by three numbers. How many possible plates start with MTU?

A domino is a rectangular tile divided into halves. On a standard double-six domino, each half contains from 0 to 6 dots, called pips. A complete set of dominoes contains one domino for each possible combination of halves. How many dominoes are in a complete set?

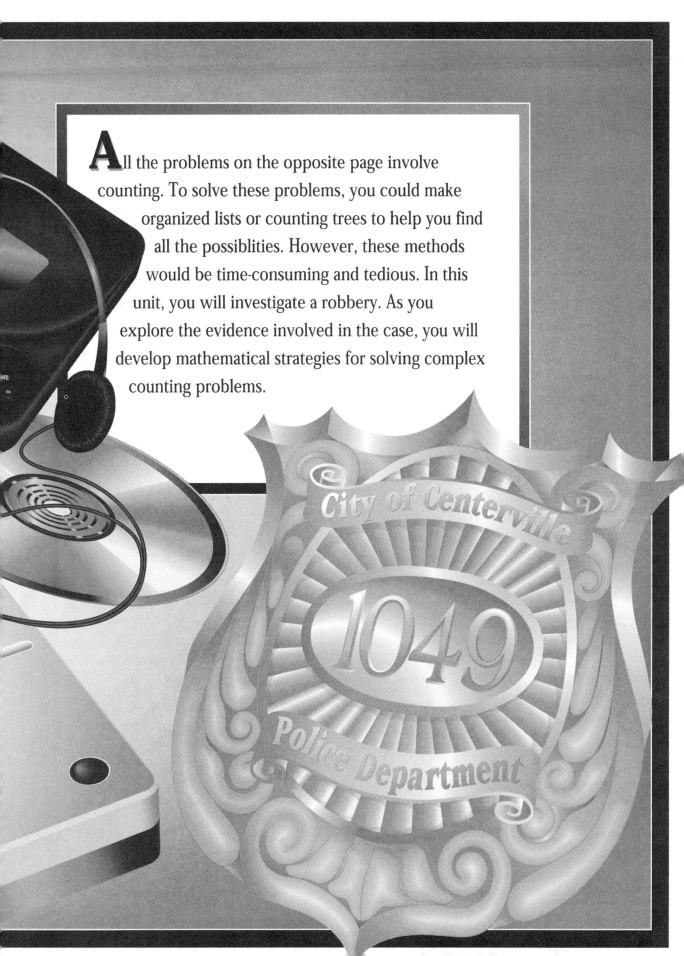

All the problems on the opposite page involve counting. To solve these problems, you could make organized lists or counting trees to help you find all the possiblities. However, these methods would be time-consuming and tedious. In this unit, you will investigate a robbery. As you explore the evidence involved in the case, you will develop mathematical strategies for solving complex counting problems.

City of Centerville

1049

Police Department

Mathematical Highlights

In *Clever Counting* you will explore some basic techniques for counting the possible outcomes of complex processes. The unit should help you to

● Recognize situations in which fundamental counting techniques apply;

● Construct organized lists and diagrams that display the outcomes of processes in systematic and easily-counted ways;

● Analyze and count paths through networks; and

● Use counting techniques to solve problems.

As you work on the problems of this unit, make it a habit to ask questions about problem situations that involve multi-step processes: *Is this a situation in which actions must take place in distinct stages to produce an outcome, with several options at each stage of the process? How many options are there at each stage? Does order of actions and choices make a difference? How could the possibilities be displayed and counted with a tree diagram, a network, or a systematic list?*

Counting Possibilities

Rodney's Radical Sounds sells radios, tape decks, and compact disc players at discount prices. There is very little room in the store to keep merchandise that is not on display, so Rodney rents a storage locker at the nearby Fail-Safe storage warehouse.

One afternoon, Rodney went to his locker and discovered that a box of expensive compact disc players was missing. He called the police, and Detective Ima Curious came to investigate.

During her initial investigation, Detective Curious gathered the following information:

- There were no signs of forced entry, and the only fingerprints on the locker were Rodney's.

- Rodney had visited his locker at noon the day before, and nothing was missing.

- The warehouse manager is on duty from 9 A.M. to 6 P.M. every day.

- Some of the lockers at Fail-Safe have push-button locks; others have combination locks. The manager keeps a list of all the combinations hidden in his office.

- The night security guard was on duty from 9 P.M. to 6 A.M. The manager suspects that the guard committed the robbery. He thinks the guard tried various combinations until the lock opened.

- The security guard said that, although she makes frequent rounds of the warehouse to inspect the locks and doors, she does not pass every locker on every trip through the warehouse.

- The security guard admitted that she was visited by a friend from 9:30 P.M. until about 11:30 P.M. She and her friend played dominoes for about an hour. After the friend left, the guard conducted a half-hour check of the warehouse.

- The guard's friend said that as he was leaving the warehouse, a van raced out of the parking lot with its lights off. He thought this was odd, so he tried to read the license plate. He could see that it was an in-state plate and contained the letters MTU, in that order. As the van passed under a street light, the friend caught a glimpse of the driver. He is certain the driver was a man.

Think about this!

Based on this information, whom, if anyone, do you suspect of committing the robbery? What questions would you like to ask Rodney, the manager, the night guard, the guard's friend, or the detective?

1.1 Making Faces

Detective Curious asked the guard's friend to work with a police artist to create a sketch of the man driving the van. To make an accurate sketch, the artist gave the witness choices for several facial features. For example, she asked, "What did his nose look like? Was it hooked? Long and straight? Turned up? Broken?"

Here are the choices the artist gave the witness:

Hair	Eyes	Nose
bushy	staring	hooked
bald	beady	long and straight
	droopy	turned up
	wide open	broken

A. How many facial descriptions can you make by choosing one attribute for each feature?

B. The witness said he remembered something distinctive about the driver's mouth. The artist suggested these possibilities:

Mouth
thin and mean
toothless
sinister grin

If you consider the hair, eyes, nose, and mouth, how many facial descriptions can you make by choosing one attribute for each feature?

▪ Problem 1.1 Follow-Up

1. Of all the facial descriptions you found in part B, how many include droopy eyes?

2. Of all the facial descriptions you found in part B, how many include a bald head and a thin, mean mouth?

1.2 Checking Plate Numbers

The witness claimed that he saw the license plate of the van. He said that it was an in-state plate containing the letter sequence MTU. In the state in which the robbery took place, license plates contain three letters followed by three numbers. How might this information help the detective solve her case?

Problem 1.2

Detective Curious wants to run each possible plate number through the computer to find out whether the registered owner has a criminal record. It takes about 20 seconds to check each plate number. How many possible plates start with MTU? Do you think this is a reasonable number of plates for the detective to check?

■ Problem 1.2 Follow-Up

1. When the detective questioned him a second time, the witness said he was really only sure that the first two letters of the plate were MT. How many possible license plates start with MT? How does this compare to the number of possible plates that start with MTU?

2. In a neighboring state, license plates have four letters followed by two numbers. Is the number of possible plates for this state greater than, less than, or equal to the number of possible plates for the state in which the crime took place? Explain your answer.

As you work on these ACE questions, use your calculator whenever you need it.

Applications

1. Makoto is getting dressed for school. The counting tree below shows his choices for shoes, pants, and shirts.

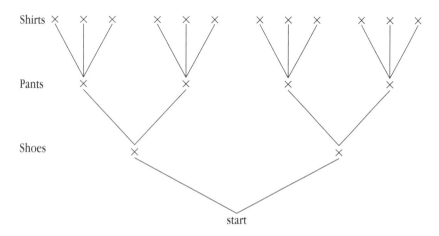

a. How many pairs of shoes does Makoto have to choose from?

b. How many pairs of pants does he have to choose from?

c. How many shirts does he have to choose from?

d. How many different combinations of shoes, pants, and a shirt can Makoto put together from these choices?

e. How can you find the answer to part d without counting each path in the diagram?

2. Ms. Suárez is choosy about what she eats. When she buys lunch in the company cafeteria, she considers only these options:

Main course   **Drink**   **Dessert**
salad   milk   fruit
pizza   orange juice   frozen yogurt
turkey sandwich   pie
        pudding

a. List four lunches Ms. Suárez might purchase. Each lunch should consist of one main course, one drink, and one dessert.

b. Copy and complete this tree diagram to show all the lunches Ms. Suárez might purchase.

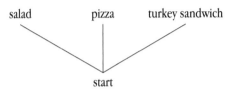

c. How many days can Ms. Suárez buy lunch in the cafeteria without having the same lunch twice?

3. At the meeting of the Future Teachers of America, ice cream cones were served. There were two kinds of cones, five flavors of ice cream, and three types of sprinkles. Each member chose one cone, one ice cream flavor, and one type of sprinkles. How many combinations were possible? Show your work.

4. Look back at the lists of hair, eyes, nose, and mouth attributes in Problem 1.1. The witness told the artist that he was sure the driver of the van was not bald. He was also certain that the driver did not have droopy eyes, a broken nose, or a sinister grin. If you eliminate these choices from the lists of attributes, how many descriptions can you make from the choices that remain?

5. In a particular counting tree, four branches extend from the starting point. At the second level, five branches extend from each branch from the previous level. At the third level, three branches extend from each branch from the previous level. How many paths through the branches of the tree are possible?

6. License plates in the state where the locker robbery took place contain three letters followed by three numbers. In Problem 1.2, you found that this scheme provides enough plates for over 17 million cars. In states with small populations, such as Alaska, North Dakota, Wyoming, and Vermont, fewer than 1 million cars are registered.

  a. Suppose you are in charge of developing a license-plate scheme for a state with a million registered cars. Describe a scheme that would provide enough plates for all the cars and require the fewest characters.

  b. Can you think of another acceptable scheme that would use the same number of characters as the scheme you described in part a? Explain.

7. If a state's motorcycle plates contain four letters, such as ABCD or MIKE, how many plates are possible?

8. If a state's license plates contain three numbers followed by four letters, such as 543 JOHE or 112 BETY, how many plates are possible?

Connections

9. Suppose the witness remembers the three letters and the first two numbers of the van's license plate and guesses the last number. What is the probability that his guess will be correct? Explain your answer.

10. Suppose the witness recalls that the driver had bushy hair and beady eyes and guesses what his nose looked like. Can you determine the probability that his guess will be correct? Explain your answer.

11. U.S. postal zip codes have two forms. The short form is a five-digit number, such as 54494. The longer form, called zip+4, has 9 digits, such as 48824-1027.

    a. What is the short form for your zip code?

    b. How many short-form zip codes are possible?

    c. How many zip+4 zip codes are possible?

    d. The U.S. population is about 260 million people. How does the number of possible zip+4 codes compare with the number of people in the United States?

12. **a.** Suppose it takes 3 seconds to manufacture a license plate. How much time would it take to manufacture every possible plate with three letters followed by three numbers? Assume the plates are made one at a time on a continuous production line. Express your answer in each of these units:

        i. seconds   **ii.** minutes   **iii.** hours

        iv. days   **v.** weeks   **vi.** years

    b. Make a table and a graph to show how the manufacturing time in hours varies with the number of license plates produced.

    c. Write an equation that shows how the manufacturing time relates to the number of license plates produced. Explain what each part of your equation means in terms of the situation.

13. If you held the letter U up to a mirror, its reflection would also be a U.

    a. List all the capital letters with this reflection property.

    b. The reflection of UTM in a mirror would be MTU. How many three-letter combinations have reflections that are also three-letter combinations?

Extensions

14. In the Clue® board game, players try to solve a murder mystery. To win, a player must identify the murderer, the murder weapon, and the room in which the murder was committed. Amadi claims that there are 118 possible solutions to the game. His sister Ayana, who has never played the game, says she can't believe this is true. Why does she say this?

In 15–18, use a current almanac to help you answer the question.

15. In Texas, license plates have four letters followed by three numbers. What is the ratio of the number of possible plates to the state's population?

16. In Michigan, license plates have three letters followed by three numbers or three numbers followed by three letters. What is the ratio of the number of possible plates to the state's population?

17. In Alaska, license plates have three letters followed by three numbers. What is the ratio of the number of possible plates to the state's population?

18. In Utah, license plates have three letters followed by three numbers. What is the ratio of the number of possible plates to the state's population?

19. **a.** Suppose a country's postal codes consist of two characters. A code may have two letters, two numbers, or a letter and a number. How many two-character codes are possible? Consider A3 to be different from 3A.

b. Suppose a country's postal codes consist of three characters. A code may have three letters, three numbers, or a combination of letters and numbers. How many three-character codes are possible?

c. Suppose a country's postal codes have six characters that are a mixture of letters and numbers, such as CB2 1QA, 3B2 A3H, and V6J 1Z8. How many six-character codes are possible?

Mathematical Reflections

In this investigation, you developed strategies for counting in situations in which there are many possibilities. These questions will help you summarize what you have learned:

1 Suppose you are given a list of options in each of several categories. You are to choose one option from each category. Describe how you could make a counting tree to help you find all the possible combinations of options. Use an example if it helps you to explain your thinking.

2 Suppose you must choose one option from each of three categories. The first category has two options, the second has three options, and the third has three options. Describe how you could list all the possible combinations without using a counting tree. Use an example if it helps you to explain your thinking.

3 In counting situations in which there are many possibilities, making a counting tree or a list can be time-consuming and cumbersome. In these cases, you can do calculations to find the number of possibilities. Look back at your work in this investigation. Find an example of a counting problem you solved by doing calculations. Describe the problem, and explain the strategy you used to find your answer.

Think about your answers to these questions, discuss your ideas with other students and your teacher, and then write a summary of your findings in your journal.

Imagine that you are writing a mystery story about a detective's investigation of a crime. What type of crime would you write about? Describe some of the characters you might include. What situations could you include in your story that would require the detective to count possibilities? You will continue to brainstorm about your story at the end of each investigation.

INVESTIGATION 2

Opening Locks

The manager of Fail-Safe suspects that the security guard stole Rodney's CD players. He suggested to Detective Curious that the guard had tried different combinations until the lock opened. The detective wondered how long it would take to try every possible combination.

2.1 Pushing Buttons

Some of the lockers at Fail-Safe have push-button locks that consist of five lettered buttons.

To open a push-button lock, the letters must be pressed in the correct sequence.

Problem 2.1

A lock sequence may have two, three, four, or five letters. A letter may not occur more than once in a sequence.

A. How many two-letter sequences are possible?

B. How many three-letter sequences are possible?

C. How many four-letter sequences are possible?

D. How many five-letter sequences are possible?

E. The security guard would not have known whether the sequence that would open Rodney's lock consisted of two, three, four, or five letters. How many possible lock sequences might she have had to try?

1. How long do you think it would take to try every possible lock sequence? Explain how you made your estimate.

2. Based on your work, do you think it is likely that someone opened Rodney's lock by trying all the possible lock sequences? Explain.

3. Does your answer to question 2 make you suspicious of anyone who was near the crime scene? Explain.

2.2 Dialing Combinations

The detective was trying to make her case based on the push-button lock data when she discovered that Rodney's locker has a *combination* lock!

The combination locks at Fail-Safe have combinations consisting of three numbers from 0 to 39 in a given order, such as 15-5-33 and 7-11-21. Do you think it would have been possible for someone to try every possible combination?

Problem 2.2

A. How many possible combinations are there for Rodney's lock? Assume that a number may not appear more than once in a combination.

B. How long do you think it would take someone to try all the possible combinations? Explain how you made your estimate.

Problem 2.2 Follow-Up

1. The detective started to list the possible lock combinations, but she soon became tired.

She then tried to make a counting tree, but she found it very tedious to draw. As she studied the patterns in her work, she had an idea:

"I can determine how many choices I have for each position in the combination. Then I can multiply those numbers together to predict the total number of possibilities!"

Do you think the detective's idea is reasonable? Why or why not?

2. For some locks, a combination may have the same number in the first and last positions but not in adjacent positions. This means that 3-1-3 is allowed, but 3-3-1 is not. If such combinations were allowed for the locks at Fail-Safe, how would the number of possible combinations for Rodney's lock change?

3. If you were in charge of security at Fail-Safe, would you recommend push-button locks or combination locks? Explain.

4. Does your work on this problem make you suspicious of anyone who was near the crime scene? Explain.

Increasing Security

In Problem 2.2, you found the number of possible combinations for a lock with 40 marks, representing the numbers from 0 to 39. Some combination locks have more or fewer than 40 marks. In this problem, you will explore the relationship between the number of marks on a lock and the number of possible combinations.

Problem 2.3

When the owner of Fail-Safe learned about the robbery, he told the manager to replace all the locks with more secure locks. However, he made it clear that he did not want to spend a lot of money. The manager did some research and found that combination locks with more marks are more expensive than locks with fewer marks. He wanted to convince the owner that the increased security provided by locks with more marks was worth the extra investment.

A. Make a table showing the number of possible combinations for locks with from 3 to 10 marks. Consider only three-number combinations with no repeated numbers. For example, to complete the row for 3 marks, consider all possible combinations of the numbers 0, 1, and 2.

Number of marks	Number of combinations
3	
4	
5	
6	
7	
8	
9	
10	

B. Use the pattern in your table to write an equation for the relationship between the number of marks, m, and the number of combinations, C.

C. Sketch a graph of your equation for m values from 3 to 10.

D. How could the manager use your graph to convince the owner to buy locks with more marks?

■ Problem 2.3 Follow-Up

1. Use your equation to find the number of possible combinations for Rodney's lock.

2. How does your answer to question 1 compare with the answer you would find by using the detective's strategy from Problem 2.2 Follow-Up?

3. a. If a lock has 40 marks and a combination consists of two numbers without repeats, how many combinations are possible? Explain your answer.

   b. If a lock has 40 marks and a combination consists of four numbers without repeats, how many combinations are possible? Explain your answer.

   c. If a lock has 20 marks and a combination consists of four numbers without repeats, how many combinations are possible? Explain your answer.

4. a. Suppose a combination consists of two numbers without repeats. Write an equation for the relationship between the number of marks, m, and the number of combinations, C.

   b. Suppose a combination consists of four numbers without repeats. Write an equation for the relationship between the number of marks, m, and the number of combinations, C.

As you work on these ACE questions, use your calculator whenever you need it.

Applications

1. Tina's new car has a push-button lock. The car is locked, and Tina has forgotten the lock sequence. She is trying to open the lock by testing each possible sequence. It takes her 5 seconds to test each sequence. The manufacturer says that there are 100,000 possible sequences.

   a. If Tina has to test every possible sequence, how many seconds will it take her to open the car door?

   b. Express your answer to part a in minutes, in hours, and in days.

   c. Make a table and a graph of the relationship between number of minutes and number of combinations tested.

   d. How could lock designers protect owners against people who might try to break into cars by trying possible lock sequences?

2. To play the Take-3 lottery game, players must choose three numbers from 0 to 30 in a particular order. The same number may appear more than once in a selection. The order of the numbers is considered, so 3-2-4 is different from 4-3-2. If a player's selection matches the winning selection, the player wins the grand prize.

   a. How many possible selections begin with 0-0?

   b. How many possible selections begin with 0-1?

   c. How many possible selections begin with 0-2?

   d. How many possible selections begin with 0-3?

e. How many possible selections begin with 0?

f. What is the total number of possible selections?

g. Freija says that if she purchases a Take-3 lottery ticket every day for a year, she is guaranteed to win at least once. Do you agree? Explain.

h. If you could write one selection every 2 seconds, how long would it take you to list all the possibilities? Express your answer in seconds, in minutes, in hours, in days, and in weeks.

3. The Guess-and-Win lottery game requires players to choose three *different* numbers from 0 to 30. The order of the numbers matters, so 3-2-4 is different from 4-3-2.

a. How many possible selections begin with 0-1?

b. How many possible selections begin with 0-2?

c. How many possible selections begin with 0-3?

d. How many possible selections begin with 0?

e. How many possible selections begin with 1?

f. What is the total number of possible selections?

4. Which of the following has the greatest number of possible combinations? Explain how you arrived at your answer.

i. a lock with 10 numbers for which a combination consists of 3 numbers with repeated numbers allowed

ii. a lock with 5 numbers for which a combination consists of 5 numbers with repeated numbers allowed

iii. a lock with 5 numbers for which a combination consists of 5 numbers with repeated numbers *not* allowed

5. Some bicycle locks are composed of several numbered wheels. To open the lock, you line up the correct sequence of numbers with the arrow.

Suppose a bicycle lock has three wheels with the numbers from 0 to 9 on each wheel.

a. List five possible combinations for this lock.

b. How many possible combinations are there? Explain how you found your answer.

6. Suppose a bicycle lock has five wheels with the numbers from 0 to 9 on each wheel. To open the lock, you line up the correct sequence of numbers with the arrow.

a. List five possible combinations for this lock.

b. How many possible combinations are there? Explain how you found your answer.

7. Suppose a lock has three wheels with the numbers from 0 to 4 on each wheel. To open the lock, you line up the correct sequence of numbers with the arrow.

   a. List five possible combinations for this lock.

   b. How many possible combinations are there? Explain how you found your answer.

Connections

8. Sammy looks in his closet and sees four shirts, three pairs of jeans, high-top tennis shoes, running shoes, and three caps. He wants to wear a shirt, a pair of jeans, shoes, and a cap. How many different outfits can he make?

9. Winona and her friends walk to the pizza parlor for dinner. They decide to order the special, a cheese pizza with one topping and a choice of crust. The choices for toppings are onions, mushrooms, green peppers, olives, pepperoni, ham, and sausage. The choices for crust are garlic, sesame seed, whole wheat, and extra crispy. How many different pizzas are possible?

Tonight's Special

A large cheese pizza with one topping and choice of crust

$8.99

10. A lock has five buttons, labeled A, B, C, D, and E. A combination consists of five letters pressed in a particular order. A letter may be repeated. Some possible combinations are A-B-A-A-E and D-D-D-D-D. How many combinations are possible?

11. a. How many different eight-letter "words" can you make by rearranging the letters in the word COMPUTER? In this situation, a "word" is any combination that includes each letter in COMPUTER exactly once. Two possible words are TRPOCMEU and ETOUMPCR.

   b. Which lock problem does this resemble? Explain.

12. Randy is helping his little sisters develop a secret code for their club. The girls want their code words to be made up of combinations of 0s and 1s, and they want to make a list of messages that correspond to the code words. For example, 01 might mean "meet me after school," and 010 might mean "bring your bike."

    a.   **i.**   How many two-digit code words are possible?

         ii.   How many three-digit code words are possible?

       iii.   How many four-digit code words are possible?

       iv.   How many *n*-digit code words are possible?

    b. Make a table and a graph and write an equation to show the relationship between the length of a code word and the number of possible code words. What kind of relationship does your graph reveal?

Extensions

13.   **a.** Find the number of possible combinations for each lock described, and tell how the two numbers compare.

      i.   a bicycle lock composed of five wheels with ten numbers on each wheel

      ii.   a bicycle lock composed of ten wheels with five numbers on each wheel

    b. Find the number of possible combinations for each lock described, and tell how the two numbers compare.

      i.   a bicycle lock composed of five wheels with *n* numbers on each wheel

      ii.   a bicycle lock composed of *n* wheels with five numbers on each wheel

14. In the Take-Your-Chances lottery game, players choose three numbers from 0 to 30 in a particular order. A number may appear more than once in a selection. To win the grand prize, a player must have selected the winning numbers in the correct order. A player wins a smaller prize if he or she has selected the winning numbers but in an incorrect order.

    a. Suppose this week's winning selection is 8-13-21. List all the selections for which a prize will be awarded.

    b. Suppose this week's winning selection is 9-18-27. List all the selections for which a prize will be awarded.

    c. If a player makes one selection for next week's game, what is the probability that he or she will win the grand prize? What is the probability that he or she will win a smaller prize?

    d. Let a, b, and c represent any three numbers. In how many different orders can a, b, and c be written?

Did you know?

Y̲ou can use the *factorial* function on your calculator to help you solve problems about combinations. The factorial symbol is an exclamation point. When an exclamation point appears after a whole number, it means "multiply all the whole numbers up to and including this number." For example, 6! represents $1 \times 2 \times 3 \times 4 \times 5 \times 6$.

The number of possible four-number combinations with no repeats that you can make from four numbers is $4 \times 3 \times 2 \times 1$. You can evaluate this by entering 4! on your calculator. What problem can you solve by entering 5! on your calculator?

Mathematical Reflections

In this investigation, you learned strategies for finding the number of possible combinations for push-button locks and combination locks. These questions will help you summarize what you have learned:

1 Suppose a lock has five numbers. How many three-number combinations are possible if repeated numbers are not allowed?

2 Suppose a lock has n numbers. How many three-number combinations are possible if repeated numbers are not allowed? Assume $n \geq 3$.

3 Suppose a lock has n numbers. How many r-number combinations are possible if repeated numbers are not allowed? Assume $n \geq r$.

4 Compare the strategies you used to find the number of possible sequences for push-button locks with the strategies you used to find the number of combinations for combination locks. Consider two types of combination locks:

- locks for which combinations with repeated numbers are not allowed

- locks for which the first and third numbers of the combination may be the same

Think about your answers to these questions, discuss your ideas with other students and your teacher, and then write a summary of your findings in your journal.

What situations might you include in your mystery story that would require the detective to estimate how long it would take to do or make something?

INVESTIGATION 3

Networks

Detective Curious decided to investigate the possibility that someone broke into the warehouse while the night guard was on duty. The guard told the detective that, although she makes frequent rounds of the warehouse to inspect the locks and doors, she does not pass every locker on every trip through the warehouse. The detective thought the thief may have hidden in Rodney's locker during the guard's rounds. If the guard did not pass Rodney's locker, she would not have noticed that the lock had been opened.

3.1 Making Rounds

The floor plan of the Fail-Safe storage warehouse is shown below. The left section contains rows of small lockers, and the right section contains rows of large lockers. During each of her inspection rounds, the guard starts at checkpoint A and walks down an aisle of small lockers to checkpoint B. From there, she walks down an aisle of large lockers to checkpoint C. One possible path is shown in the diagram.

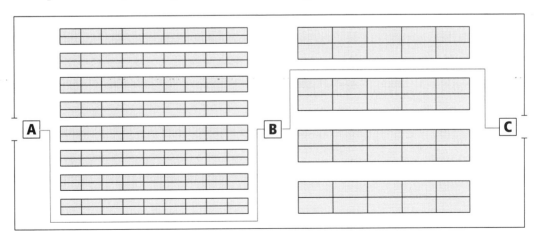

A. How many paths are there from A to B? How many paths are there from B to C?

B. How many paths are there from A to C through B? Explain your reasoning.

C. If Rodney has a small locker, how many of the paths from A to C pass by his locker?

D. If Rodney has a large locker, how many of the paths from A to C pass by his locker?

E. If Rodney has a small locker, what is the probability that the guard will *not* pass his locker on one of her rounds?

F. If Rodney has a large locker, what is the probability that the guard will *not* pass his locker on one of her rounds?

Problem 3.1 Follow-Up

1. Suppose the warehouse were laid out so that there were 15 paths from A to B and 12 paths from B to C. How would your answers to parts B–F of Problem 3.1 change?

2. Compare the method you used to count paths through the warehouse with the methods you used in previous investigations to count facial descriptions, license plates, and lock combinations.

3.2 Networking

The diagram below is a model of the floor plan of the warehouse. A diagram like this is called a **network**. A network is made up of *nodes* and *edges*. In the network below, the nodes A, B, and C represent the warehouse checkpoints, and the edges connecting the nodes represent aisles between the rows of lockers. A *path* from node A to node C consists of an edge from node A to node B followed by an edge from node B to node C.

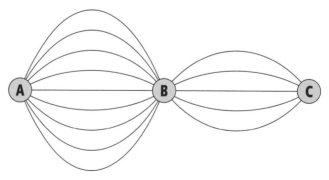

This network models the warehouse floor plan because it contains all the important information in a simplified form.

A. In this network, a single edge connects node A to node B, and 8 edges connect node B to node C. How many paths are there from node A to node C that pass through node B?

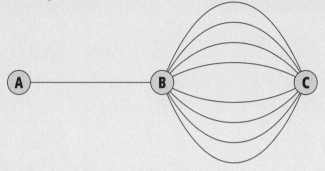

B. In this network, 2 edges connect node A to node B, and 5 edges connect node B to node C. How many paths are there from node A to node C that pass through node B?

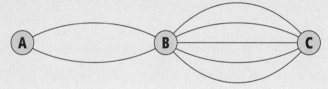

C. In another network, 25 edges connect node A to node B, and 32 edges connect node B to node C. How many paths are there from node A to node C that pass through node B? Explain your reasoning.

Problem 3.2 Follow-Up

1. For each network in Problem 3.2, find the number of different *round trips* from node A to node C and back to node A.

2. For parts A and B of Problem 3.2, describe how adding another edge connecting nodes A and B would change the number of round trips.

3.3 Designing Networks

You have found the number of paths through several networks. In this problem, you will design networks that satisfy given constraints.

Problem 3.3

A. 1. Design at least three networks with nodes A, B, and C and 12 edges. Each edge should connect node A to node B or node B to node C.

2. For each network you drew, record the number of edges from node A to node B, the number of edges from node B to node C, and the total number of paths from node A to node C. Look for a pattern in your results.

3. Use your findings from part 2 to help you draw the network with the maximum number of paths from node A to node C. Explain how you know that your network has the maximum number of paths.

B. Design a network with nodes A, B, C, and D and 12 edges that has the maximum number of paths from node A to node D through nodes B and C. How did you decide how to distribute the 12 edges?

C. Suppose you are given a specific number of nodes and a specific number of edges. How can you design a network with the maximum number of paths from the first node to the last node?

D. Describe how the numbers of edges between consecutive pairs of nodes are related to the total number of paths in a network.

■ Problem 3.3 Follow-Up

1. In the network below, how many paths are there from node A to node F?

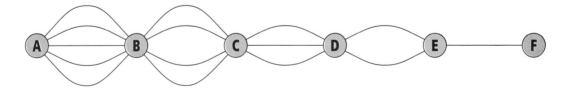

2. In the network below, the number on each edge represents the time, in seconds, it takes to travel along that edge. Which path from node A to node F will take the least amount of time to travel? Explain your answer.

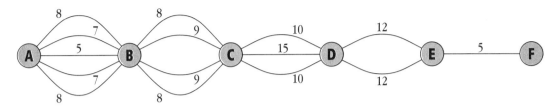

As you work on these ACE questions, use your calculator whenever you need it.

Applications

1. a. In the diagram below, how many paths are there from A to D?

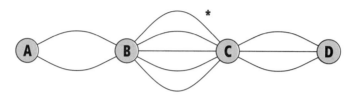

b. How many paths from A to D pass the location represented by the asterisk?

2. Design a network with 3 nodes, 11 edges, and the maximum number of paths from the first node to the last node.

3. Design a network with nodes A, B, and C and exactly 12 paths from node A to node C that pass through node B.

4. Design a network with nodes A, B, and C and exactly 11 paths from node A to node C that pass through node B.

5. If possible, design a network with nodes A, B, C, and D and exactly 6 paths from node A to node D that pass through nodes B and C. If you think this cannot be done, explain why.

6. If possible, design a network with nodes A, B, C, and D and exactly 5 paths from node A to node D that pass through nodes B and C. If you think this cannot be done, explain why.

Connections

7. Shelly wants to build a rectangular pen for her dog Sam. She has 24 meters of fencing.

    a. Draw and label some rectangles that Shelly could form with the fencing.

    b. What are the dimensions of the rectangle that would give Sam the greatest area in which to run?

    c. How is this problem similar to part A of Problem 3.3?

8. In question 7, you explored rectangles that could be constructed from 24 meters of fencing.

    a. Write an equation for the relationship between the length of one side of the rectangle and the area enclosed by the fencing.

    b. Make a graph of the relationship between the length of one side of the rectangle and the area enclosed by the fencing.

    c. What type of relationship do your graph and table represent? Explain how you know.

Extensions

9. The diagram below represents a grid of city streets. Officer Hansel is at point A when he gets a call about a crime in progress at point B.

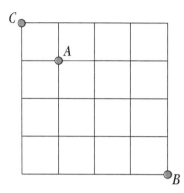
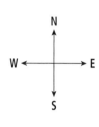

    a. List five different shortest routes that Officer Hansel could take to the crime scene. Describe each route with a string of letters specifying one-block moves. For example, Officer Hansel could go east, then south, then south, then east, then south, and then east. You would indicate this by writing ESSESE.

    b. How many different shortest routes are there? Explain.

    c. Officer Valdez is at point C. How many different shortest routes could she take to the crime scene?

10. The diagram on the next page shows the routes a professor who lives in Detroit, Michigan, could take to the University of Windsor in Ontario, Canada.

    a. Draw a simple network with nodes and edges to model this situation.

    b. Use your network to find the number of possible routes from the professor's home to the university.

c. How many different routes could the professor take from the university to her home?

d. How many different round-trip routes could the professor make between her home and the university?

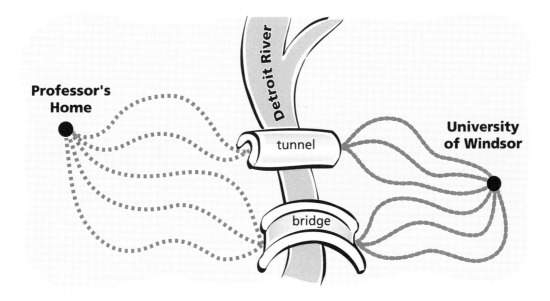

Mathematical Reflections

In this investigation, you explored the number of paths through given networks, and you designed networks that satisfied given conditions. These questions will help you summarize what you have learned:

1 How is finding the number of possible paths through a network similar to finding the number of possible lock combinations? How is it different?

2 **a.** Write a problem whose solution involves evaluating $5 \times 4 \times 3$.

b. Write a problem whose solution involves evaluating $20 \times 20 \times 20$.

3 Suppose you wanted to design a network with nodes A, B, and C; n edges; and the maximum number of paths from node A to node C through node B. How should you arrange the edges?

Think about your answers to these questions, discuss your ideas with other students and your teacher, and then write a summary of your findings in your journal.

In your mystery story, what situation might you include that would require the detective to find the number of paths through a network?

Deciding Whether Order Is Important

Detective Curious considered the possibility that the locker robbery may have taken place while the security guard and her friend were playing dominoes. She reasoned that they may have been so involved in their game that they would not have noticed a disturbance among the lockers.

4.1 Playing Dominoes

A domino is a rectangular tile divided into halves. On a standard *double-six* domino, each half contains from 0 to 6 dots, called *pips*. A complete set of dominoes contains one domino for each possible combination of halves.

Problem 4.1

A. How many different dominoes are in a complete set?

B. The vending machines at Fail-Safe offer seven types of sandwiches and seven different drinks. The security guard wants to buy one sandwich and one drink. From how many combinations can she choose?

C. The security guard in a nearby storage warehouse can follow seven routes from checkpoint A to checkpoint B and seven routes from checkpoint B to checkpoint C. How many routes can he follow from checkpoint A to checkpoint C through checkpoint B?

D. Parts A–C each involve finding the number of ways to fill two positions when there are seven choices for each position. Compare the strategies you used to answer each part. How are the strategies similar? How are they different?

■ Problem 4.1 Follow-Up

1. a. Is it possible to arrange *all* the different dominoes in a chain so that adjacent halves match and the domino half that starts the chain matches the domino half that ends the chain? If it is possible to make such a chain, give an example of a chain that works.

   b. Is there more than one way to make such a domino chain? Explain.

2. How many pips are in a set of double-six dominoes?

4.2 Choosing Locks

When you first tried to find the number of dominoes in a set, you may have counted some dominoes twice. If you used number pairs to represent the dominoes, you may have counted both 1–2 and 2–1. Because 1–2 and 2–1 represent the same domino, you need to count only one of the pairs. In counting situations like this, *order is not important*.

1–2 and 2–1 represent the same domino.

When you consider possible zip codes, however, 94601 *is* different from 19460. In this situation, *order is important*.

94601 and 19460 are zip codes for different cities

As you work on this problem and the follow-up questions, think carefully about whether the order of the choices is important.

Problem 4.2

After reviewing all he had learned about locks, the manager of Fail-Safe narrowed his choices to six models: the ACME CrimeStopper, the BurgleProof 2000, the Citadel, the Deterrent, the EverSafe, and the Fortress. He planned to bring samples of the locks to a meeting of Fail-Safe customers. Just before the meeting, he decided that offering so many choices would just confuse the customers. He chose two of the locks to bring to the meeting.

A. There are several ways the manager could have chosen the two locks. For example, he could have chosen the ACME CrimeStopper and the EverSafe. In how many different ways could the manager have chosen the two locks? Prove your answer is correct by listing all the possible pairs of locks.

B. If the manager had taken three locks to the meeting, in how many different ways could he have chosen them? Prove your answer is correct by listing all the possible sets of three locks.

C. How is finding the number of different ways the manager could have chosen the locks similar to and different from finding the number of lock combinations in Investigation 2?

▨ Problem 4.2 Follow-Up

1. Six students are competing in the 100-meter dash. How many different arrangements of first-place, second-place, and third-place finishers are there?

2. How is question 1 similar to part B of Problem 4.2? How is it different?

As you work on these ACE questions, use your calculator whenever you need it.

Applications

1. Suppose a special type of dominoes has from 0 to 8 pips on each half. How many different dominoes would be in a complete set?

2. Anya is forming a chain of double-six dominoes like the one described in Problem 4.1 Follow-Up. She started with the domino shown below. Now she must select a domino to connect to either side of this one. How many dominoes does she have to choose from? Remember, adjacent domino halves must match.

3. a. In how many different ways can two locks be chosen from a set of four locks?

   b. In how many different ways can two locks be chosen from a set of five locks?

   c. In how many different ways can two locks be chosen from a set of seven locks?

   d. Look at your answers to parts a–c and Problem 4.2. Describe a pattern you could use to predict the number of different ways two locks can be chosen from a set of n locks.

Connections

4. Kyle just bought a new car. His friends Alexis, Bob, Carlos, Emile, and Frankie all want to ride with him to the football game, but he can take only three people with him.

    a. Kyle decides to choose three friends by randomly drawing names. He writes the five names on slips of paper and puts them in his cap. In how many ways can he choose three of the five friends?

    b. What is the probability that he will choose Alexis, Carlos, and Emile?

5.   **a.** Al, Betty, and Conrado meet and shake hands. If each person shakes hands with everyone else, how many handshakes take place? Explain.

    b. Al, Betty, Conrado, and Ezra meet and shake hands. If each person shakes hands with everyone else, how many handshakes take place? Explain.

    c. Twenty people meet and shake hands. If each person shakes hands with everyone else, how many handshakes take place? Explain.

    d. How is finding the number of handshakes exchanged among a group of people similar to finding the number of different dominoes in a set? How is it different?

    e. How is finding the number of handshakes exchanged among a group of people similar to finding the number of two-number lock combinations? How is it different?

6.   **a.** Before the championship match, the four members of the East High quiz-bowl team exchanged handshakes with the four members of the West High team. Each member of one team shook hands with each member of the other team. How many handshakes took place?

b. The seven members of the North High debate team shook hands with the seven members of the South High team. Each member of one team shook hands with each member of the other team. How many handshakes took place?

c. The nine members of the Miller Middle School swim team exchanged high fives with one another after Tuesday's meet. How many high fives took place?

d. Which of the problems in parts a–c is most similar to finding the number of different dominoes in a set? Explain your answer.

e. Which of the problems in parts a–c is most similar to finding the number of two-number combinations for a push-button lock with repeats allowed? Explain your answer.

7. Donae made a chart to help her find the number of different dominoes in a set.

	0	1	2	3	4	5	6
0	(0, 0)	(0, 1)	(0, 2)	(0, 3)	(0, 4)	(0, 5)	(0, 6)
1	(1, 0)	(1, 1)	(1, 2)	(1, 3)	(1, 4)	(1, 5)	(1, 6)
2	(2, 0)	(2, 1)	(2, 2)	(2, 3)	(2, 4)	(2, 5)	(2, 6)
3	(3, 0)	(3, 1)	(3, 2)	(3, 3)	(3, 4)	(3, 5)	(3, 6)
4	(4, 0)	(4, 1)	(4, 2)	(4, 3)	(4, 4)	(4, 5)	(4, 6)
5	(5, 0)	(5, 1)	(5, 2)	(5, 3)	(5, 4)	(5, 5)	(5, 6)
6	(6, 0)	(6, 1)	(6, 2)	(6, 3)	(6, 4)	(6, 5)	(6, 6)

a. What do the number pairs on the diagonal represent?

b. Do (2, 3) and (3, 2) represent the same domino or different dominoes?

c. How are the dominoes represented by pairs *above* the diagonal related to the dominoes represented by pairs *below* the diagonal?

d. Explain how you could use the chart to find the number of different dominoes in a set.

e. Write a general equation for the number of different dominoes, *d*, in a set if each domino has from 0 to *n* pips on each half.

8. The chart in question 7 can also represent the number of handshakes exchanged among a group of seven people. Use this interpretation of the chart to answer parts a–d.

   a. What do the number pairs on the diagonal represent?

   b. What do the pairs (2, 3) and (3, 2) represent?

   c. How many different handshakes are represented in the chart? Explain.

   d. Write a general equation for the number of handshakes, h, exchanged among n people.

9. Kari drew this diagram to help her visualize the problem of counting the dominoes in a set of double-six dominoes. The diagram leads to a general equation for the number of different dominoes, d, in a set if each domino has from 0 to n pips on each half.

Diagram	**General Equation**
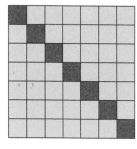	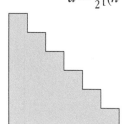 $d = \frac{1}{2}[(n + 1)^2 - (n + 1)] + n + 1$

   a. How might Kari have been thinking about the problem?

   b. Explain how her diagram leads to the general equation.

   c. Describe the shape of the graph of the general equation.

Extensions

In 10–14, use the following information: The tiles in the Tri-Ominoes® game are shaped like triangles. Each corner of a tile contains the number 0, 1, 2, 3, 4, or 5. A Tri-Ominoes game contains a tile for every combination of three numbers.

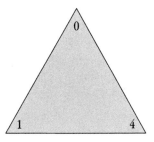 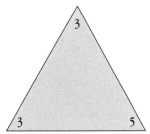

10. How many tiles contain exactly two 1s? Explain how you found your answer.

11. How many tiles contain exactly one 1? Explain how you found your answer.

12. How many tiles contain at least one 1? Explain how you found your answer.

13. How many tiles contain at least one 2? Explain how you found your answer.

14. Find the error in this argument: There are 21 Tri-Ominoes tiles that contain 1s. There must also be 21 tiles that contain 0s, 21 tiles that contain 2s, 21 tiles that contain 3s, and so on. So, the total number of tiles must be 6 × 21, or 126.

Mathematical Reflections

In this investigation, you found the number of dominoes in a set and the number of ways a given number of locks can be chosen from a set of six locks. You discovered that in these counting situations, order is not important. These questions will help you summarize what you have learned:

1 **a.** In some counting situations, order is important. For example, when counting possible lock combinations, 2-3-4 is different from 3-4-2. Give two more examples of counting situations in which order is important.

b. Explain why order is important in your examples.

2 **a.** In some counting situations, order is not important. For example, when counting combinations of pizza toppings, a mushroom-and-onion pizza is the same as an onion-and-mushroom pizza. Give two more examples of counting situations in which order is not important.

b. Explain why order is not important in your examples.

Think about your answers to these questions, discuss your ideas with other students and your teacher, and then write a summary of your findings in your journal.

In your mystery story, what counting situations might your detective encounter in which order is not important?

Wrapping Things Up

In the previous investigations, you learned techniques for solving counting problems. In this investigation, you will use what you have learned to help Detective Curious investigate a second robbery.

5.1 Catching a Bicycle Thief

Detective Curious was narrowing in on a suspect when another robbery took place at Fail-Safe. The detective was called to the scene on the morning the second burglary was discovered. During her investigation, she gathered the following information:

- Three mountain bikes were stolen from a locker rented by Bagged Bikes, Inc. The locker has a push-button lock with five buttons.

- The warehouse manager suspects that the night security guard committed the crime. The guard was on duty alone for several hours the night of the robbery. The guard claims she is innocent.

- There is an emergency exit at the end of the aisle in which Bagged Bikes' locker is located. The detective discovered tape over the latch of the exit, which prevented the door from closing properly.

- When the detective went to the manager's home to question him, she noticed a new mountain bike just inside his apartment door. The bike was the same model as one of the stolen bikes. The manager pointed out that mountain bikes are very popular and that many people own them.

• When the owner of Bagged Bikes checked the serial numbers for the stolen bikes, she found that the records had been smudged. She knew that each serial number consisted of three letters followed by six numbers, but she could read only the first two letters and the last four numbers of each.

Model	Serial number
Rocky Road	UM꞉ꞏ ꞉3245
Trail Blazer	UM꞉꞉ ꞏ4397
Rugged Rider	UM꞉ ꞉ꞏ7711

Problem 5.1

You know as much as the detective does about counting combinations and calculating probabilities. Imagine that the detective asks you to help her with the case.

A. Which pieces of evidence would you investigate further? How would you proceed with your investigation?

B. What questions would you ask the security guard, the manager, or someone else involved in the case?

C. Does the evidence from the second robbery clear any of the suspects? Who are your suspects now? Why?

■ Problem 5.1 Follow-Up

1. a. One of the smudged serial numbers was UM _ _ _ 7711. The first blank represents a letter, and the other two blanks represent numbers. In how many ways can this serial number be completed?

 b. The bike at the manager's home had the serial number UMZ567711. Based on your findings from part a, can you draw any conclusions about the manager's guilt or innocence? Explain.

2. a. Assume that all mountain bikes have serial numbers with three letters followed by six numbers. How many possible combinations are there for the first two letters and the last four numbers of the serial number for a mountain bike?

b. What are the chances that the serial number on the manager's bike would contain the sequence UM_ _ _ 7711?

c. Based on your findings, can you draw any conclusions about the manager's guilt or innocence? Explain.

As you work on these ACE questions, use your calculator whenever you need it.

Applications

1. Detective Curious took her team of detectives out for ice cream. The ice cream shop offers 12 flavors of ice cream.

Apple crisp	Eggnog	Italian raspberry
Banana nut	French vanilla	Jalapeño pepper
Chocolate	Gooey caramel	Kiwi
Date swirl	Heavenly peach	Lemon sherbet

A single scoop of ice cream costs $1.25, and two scoops cost $1.75. A cup or a sugar cone is included in the price of the ice cream; a waffle cone is 25¢ extra.

a. How many different one-scoop orders are possible?

b. How many different $2 orders are possible?

c. How many different $1.75 orders are possible?

In 2–6, use this information: To keep data on computer networks secure, many computer systems require users to enter a password.

2. If a computer system accepts only three-digit passwords, such as 314 or 007, how many passwords are possible?

3. If a computer system accepts only passwords consisting of one letter followed by three numbers, such as Z300 and E271, how many passwords are possible?

4. If a computer system accepts only two-letter passwords, such as AZ and CC, how many passwords are possible?

5. If a computer system accepts only passwords consisting of two letters followed by three numbers, such as AB123 and LP333, how many passwords are possible?

6. The computer system at Jamie's school accepts only six-character passwords. A password may be all letters, all numbers, or a combination of numbers and letters. For example, A23BC7 and JTFEY1 are possible passwords. Jamie forgot his password and is attempting to log onto the system by guessing six-character sequences. How many such combinations are possible?

Connections

7. Akili, Beatrice, Consuelo, and David eat lunch together every day.

    a. Use the letters A, B, C, and D to represent the students. List all the possible orders in which the four students could stand in the lunch line.

    b. Make a counting tree for finding all the possible orders in which the four students could stand in the lunch line. How many paths are there through the branches of your tree?

    c. If Elena joined the students for lunch, in how many possible orders could the five students stand in line?

8. When counting two-choice combinations, it often helps to make a chart like the one below. Detective Curious made this chart to help her assign tasks to her detectives. The names of the detectives are listed across the top of the chart, and the tasks are listed along the side. Each box in the chart represents a possible assignment. The mark indicates that Clouseau has been assigned the task of gathering descriptions.

	Clouseau	Hercule	Jane	Sherlock	Jessica
determining lock combinations					
investigating license plates					
conducting interviews					
gathering descriptions	✓				
researching phone numbers					

a. In how many ways can Detective Curious make the assignments if each detective is to have a different task?

b. What other method could you use to count the possible ways to assign the tasks?

c. Would this type of chart be useful for counting the number of different faces a police artist could draw by combining eye, nose, hair, and mouth attributes? Explain.

d. Would this type of chart be useful for counting the number of possible three-number lock combinations? Explain.

9. Mr. Saari makes a chart each semester for recording grades. He writes student names down the left column of the chart, and lists assignments, tests, quizzes, and projects along the top.

	Q1	Q2	Test 1	Proj 1
L. Alavosus	18	24	85	93
D. Alvarez	23	21	81	100
N. Chan	21	15	92	89

a. Next semester, Mr. Saari plans to give 5 quizzes, 3 tests, 10 homework assignments, and 3 projects. How many columns will he need to record all the scores?

b. If Mr. Saari has 28 students, how many score boxes will be filled at the end of the semester? Assume he will record a 0 for any missed or incomplete assignment, quiz, test, or project.

c. **i.** If Mr. Saari has 35 students, how many score boxes will be filled at the end of the semester?

   ii. Would adding one student or adding one test cause the greater increase in the number of score boxes filled?

10. Write a problem that could be answered by using this counting tree. Copy the counting tree, and label it to represent the solution to your problem.

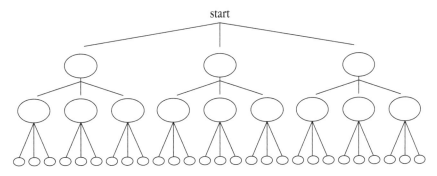

11. Write a problem that could be answered by using this counting tree. Copy the counting tree, and label it to represent the solution to your problem.

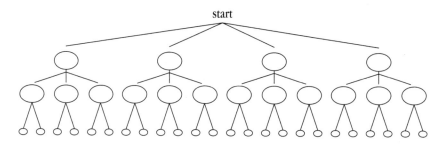

Extensions

In 12–16, use this information: In North America, a telephone number consists of a three-digit *area code*, followed by a three-digit *prefix*, followed by four more digits. For example, the telephone number of the White House in Washington, D.C., is (202) 456-1111.

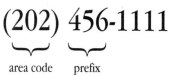

The first digit of an area code and the first digit of a prefix must be greater than or equal to 2.

12. How many telephone numbers with an area code of 500 are possible?

13. Toll-free telephone numbers have an area code of 800 or 888. How many toll-free telephone numbers are possible?

14. How many telephone numbers with the same area code and prefix as your telephone number are possible?

15. How many different U.S. telephone numbers are possible?

16. Telephone numbers mentioned in television shows and movies have the prefix 555. No actual phone numbers have this prefix. If you exclude phone numbers with the prefix 555, how many different U.S. phone numbers are possible?

Did you know?

As people within a particular area code add telephone lines for computer modems, fax machines, and cellular phones, more and more telephone numbers are needed. When all the possible numbers for an area code are taken, a new area code must be instituted. Until recently, all area codes started with digits from 2 to 9 and had 0 or 1 as the second digit. Now area codes can be any three-digit combination with a first digit greater than or equal to 2 except 411, 611, and 911.

---

17. A traveling salesman is trying to plan the least expensive route for visiting his customers. He needs to stop in ten cities on his trip. He can visit the cities in any order, but he doesn't want to visit the same city twice. He decides to list the cities in every possible order and then check the travel costs for each possibility.

a. Do you think the salesman's plan of figuring out the cost for each possibility is a good one? Explain.

b. Do you think a counting tree would help the salesman with his plan? Explain.

Mathematical Reflections

In this unit, you learned techniques for counting the number of ways a group of choices can be made or a set of positions can be filled. These questions will help you summarize what you have learned:

1 Identify the choices or positions involved in each counting problem.

   a. finding the number of faces the police artist could draw (Problem 1.1)

   b. finding the number of license plates with three letters followed by three numbers (Problem 1.2)

   c. finding the number of three-number lock combinations (Problem 2.2)

   d. finding the number of paths through a network (Problem 3.2)

   e. finding the number of dominoes in a set (Problem 4.1)

2 State a rule or rules for finding the number of ways a group of choices could be made or a set of positions could be filled.

3 Explain how you can find the number of possibilities represented by a counting tree without counting the last set of branches.

4 A particular counting problem involves making three choices in order. There are a options for the first choice, b options for the second choice, and c options for the third choice. Explain how you would find the number of possible combinations of options.

Think about your answers to these questions, discuss your ideas with other students and your teacher, and then write a summary of your findings in your journal.

Describe how the detective in your story might use charts, graphs, or counting trees to explain his or her solution.

Complete one of the projects described below.

Project 1: Writing a Detective Story

Throughout this unit, you have been recording ideas for a mystery story. Use your ideas to write a story about a detective's investigation of a crime. Your story should include some of the following:

- a cast of suspicious characters
- a detective with mathematical ability and an assistant who always needs explanations
- a lock combination
- a getaway vehicle
- different getaway routes
- a partially legible telephone number found at the scene of the crime

Your story must show the detective doing the following:

- counting combinations
- figuring out how long it would take to make, do, or check something
- using probability to show what is likely or unlikely to have happened
- using charts, graphs, or counting trees to explain his or her solution

Project 2: Making Trains

In this project, you will make "trains" by joining "cars" of different lengths. A "car" is a rectangular strip of paper; a "train" is one car or two or more cars placed end-to-end. You will find the cars on Labsheet UP. Each car is labeled with a number that indicates its length in centimeters.

For each different car, find every possible train you can make with the same length as that car. Consider trains made from the same cars, but in a different order, to be different. This means that a 1-car followed by a 2-car is different from a 2-car followed by a 1-car. The drawing below shows the four trains that can be made with the same length as a 3-car.

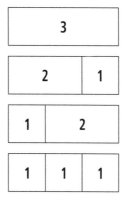

For each different car on the labsheet, record the length of the car and the number of trains with the same length as that car. Look for a pattern in your results. Write an equation for the relationship between the length of a car, L, and the number of trains with that length, N. Compare the pattern of change and the equation for this situation with the patterns and equations for other situations you have studied in this unit.

Write a paper two or three pages in length summarizing your findings.

Looking Back and Looking Ahead

Unit Reflections

Working on the problems of this unit, you have **learned strategies for counting the possibilities in complex situations. You learned how to recognize problems where** *counting* **techniques apply and how to use diagrams and tables to find patterns in counting tasks. You learned how to analyze and count paths through networks. Most important of all, you learned how to apply thinking and reasoning skills in problem situations and how to provide persuasive arguments to support your proposed solutions.**

Using Combinatorial Reasoning—To test your understanding and skill in work with counting techniques, consider the following questions about activity in a Summer Creative Arts Camp.

1 *Pat visited the camp's library and decided to select one book by each of these authors:*

J.K. Rowling books: Harry Potter and the Sorcerer's Stone, Harry Potter and the Prisoner of Azkaban, Harry Potter and the Chamber of Secrets, *and* Harry Potter and the Goblet of Fire;

Charles Dickens books: Great Expectations, Oliver Twist, *and* David Copperfield;

Mildred Taylor books: Let the Circle Be Unbroken *and* Roll of Thunder, Hear My Cry.

   a. How many different sets of books could Pat choose? Draw a counting tree that shows the selection possibilities.

   b. How many sets of books are possible if Pat chooses to read *Harry Potter and the Chamber of Secrets* as the J.K. Rowling selection?

   c. Suppose Pat chooses *Prisoner of Azkaban, Oliver Twist, and Let the Circle Be Unbroken.* In how many orders could Pat read the books, if he chose to read them one at a time?

2 *Each book in the Summer Creative Arts Camp library is coded using a pattern with groups of letters and digits like "XAN-MP-18." The first three letters identify the author. The next two letters identify the title. The last two digits identify the copy number.*

a. How many author codes are available?

b. How many title codes are available for each author?

c. How many copy codes are available for each author-title combination?

d. How many book codes are available for the library?

3 *The Creative Arts Camp is held at a university in Pat's hometown. Pat travels by bike to the library and then takes a bus to the university. There are three bike paths from Pat's home to the library and two public buses that travel from the library to the university.*

a. How many different routes can Pat take from home to the university? How many from the university to Pat's home?

b. During the second week of the program, Pat learned that the university has its own shuttle that carries passengers from the library to the university with no stops in between. How many routes are available from Pat's home to the university if that shuttle is used?

4 *The Summer Creative Arts Camp offers classes in drama, music, creative writing, reading, photography, and painting. There are four class periods each day.*

a. How many different class schedules are possible for the campers if no subject is taken more than once in a day?

b. If all students take reading as their first class, how many class schedules are possible?

5 *At the end of the summer camp, students submit their work for judging by the camp teachers. Prizes are awarded for first, second, and third place in each of the six subject areas. There are 60 students attending the camp, and 10 are from Pat's school.*

a. In how many ways could students from Pat's school win all three prizes in drama?

b. In how many ways could the top two prizes in photography be awarded to students who are *not* from Pat's school?

c. If one student is randomly selected to win a book signed by his or her favorite contemporary author, what is the probability that the lucky student will be from Pat's school? What is the probability that the lucky student will *not* be from Pat's school?

Explaining Your Reasoning—To solve the problems about activities at the Summer Creative Arts Camp, you needed to use counting strategies. When you use such mathematical calculations to solve a problem or make a decision, it is important to be able to justify each step in your reasoning.

1. What general counting idea is needed to answer questions such as those in Problems 1–5, without simply listing all possibilities? How could you use a diagram to persuade someone that the counting idea is correct?

2. How is the general counting technique adjusted for questions where

    a. the order of action or selection matters or doesn't matter?

    b. repeats are not allowed?

The counting ideas and techniques used in this unit will be applied and extended in future mathematics classes and in other work on problems of science and mathematics, especially those that involve probability. Clever counting will often help you figure out the number of possible actions in a situation that at first may seem very complex.

counting tree A diagram that shows all the possible ways a set of choices—each with one or more options—can be made. The counting tree below shows the possible three-number lock sequences for a push-button lock with three buttons—labeled 1, 2, and 3—if repeated numbers are not allowed.

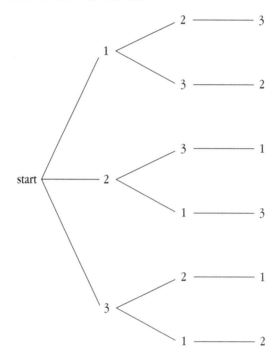

network A collection of points, or nodes, connected by edges. The network on the left has two nodes and three edges. The network on the right has four nodes and five edges. In this unit, you found the number of paths through a network. For example, in the network on the right, there are four paths from node A to node D.

Index